How to Be an Empathetic Leader: A Comprehensive Guide

By Kenan Byrd

Table of Contents

1. Introduction to Empathetic Leadership

2. Understanding Empathy

3. The Benefits of Empathetic Leadership

4. Developing Self-Awareness

5. Active Listening and Communication

6. Building Trust and Authentic Relationships

7. Emotional Intelligence in Leadership

8. Fostering a Positive Work Environment

Chapter 1: Introduction to Empathetic Leadership

What is Empathetic Leadership?

Empathetic leadership is the practice of understanding and sharing the feelings, perspectives, and experiences of others within a leadership context. It goes beyond traditional leadership methods by prioritizing emotional connections and fostering a culture of compassion and respect. Empathetic leaders strive to understand their team members' viewpoints, create an inclusive environment, and respond with genuine care and support.

Why Empathy Matters in Leadership

Empathy in leadership is crucial for several reasons:

1. Enhanced Communication: Empathetic leaders listen actively, ensuring that team members feel heard and understood. This fosters open and honest communication.

2. Increased Trust: By demonstrating empathy, leaders build trust with their team, leading to stronger relationships and loyalty.
3. Improved Morale: An empathetic approach creates a positive work environment, boosting employee morale and job satisfaction.
4. Better Decision Making: Understanding different perspectives allows leaders to make more informed and balanced decisions.
5. Higher Productivity: When employees feel valued and supported, they are more engaged and productive.

The Journey Ahead

In this book, we will explore the various aspects of empathetic leadership, from understanding empathy itself to practical strategies for developing and sustaining empathy in your leadership style. Each chapter will provide insights, techniques, and real-life examples to help you become a more empathetic leader.

Chapter 2: Understanding Empathy

Defining Empathy

Empathy is the ability to understand and share the feelings of another person. It involves recognizing emotions in others, imagining what they are experiencing, and responding with compassion. Empathy can be broken down into three types:

1. Cognitive Empathy: Understanding someone else's perspective or mental state.
2. Emotional Empathy: Sharing the emotional experience of another person.
3. Compassionate Empathy: Recognizing someone's emotional state and taking action to help.

The Science of Empathy

Research shows that empathy is rooted in our brain's neural circuitry. Mirror neurons, for instance, play a key role in how we understand and mimic the emotions and actions of others. This biological basis highlights that empathy is a natural human capability that can be nurtured and developed.

Empathy vs. Sympathy

While empathy involves feeling with someone, sympathy is feeling for someone. Sympathy often entails pity or sorrow for someone else's misfortune, which can create distance between individuals. Empathy, on the other hand, bridges that gap by fostering connection and understanding.

Developing Empathy

Empathy can be cultivated through intentional practices:

1. Active Listening: Pay close attention to what others are saying without interrupting.
2. Mindfulness: Stay present in conversations and observe emotional cues.
3. Perspective-Taking: Try to see situations from others' viewpoints.
4. Emotional Regulation: Manage your own emotions to respond appropriately to others.

Chapter 3: The Benefits of Empathetic Leadership

Enhanced Team Collaboration

Empathetic leaders encourage a collaborative environment where team members feel comfortable sharing ideas and feedback. This leads to more innovative solutions and a stronger sense of community.

Increased Employee Engagement

When employees feel understood and valued, they are more likely to be engaged in their work. Empathetic leaders create a supportive atmosphere that motivates team members to contribute their best efforts.

Reduced Conflict

By understanding and addressing the underlying emotions and concerns of team members, empathetic leaders can resolve conflicts more effectively. This proactive approach minimizes misunderstandings and fosters a harmonious workplace.

Improved Retention Rates

Employees who feel supported and appreciated by their leaders are less likely to leave their organization. Empathy in leadership can reduce turnover rates and retain top talent.

Positive Organizational Culture

Empathetic leadership promotes a culture of respect, inclusion, and kindness. This positive environment not only benefits employees but also enhances the organization's reputation and attractiveness to potential hires.

Chapter 4: Developing Self-Awareness

The Role of Self-Awareness in Empathetic Leadership

Self-awareness is the foundation of empathetic leadership. It involves recognizing your own emotions, strengths, weaknesses, and how they impact others. A self-aware leader can regulate their emotions, make thoughtful decisions, and connect more deeply with their team.

Techniques for Enhancing Self-Awareness

1. Reflection: Regularly reflect on your actions, decisions, and their effects on others.
2. Feedback: Seek feedback from colleagues, mentors, and team members to gain different perspectives.
3. Mindfulness Practices: Engage in mindfulness activities such as meditation to stay present and aware of your emotional state.
4. Journaling: Write about your experiences and emotions to gain insights into your behavior and patterns.

The Impact of Self-Awareness on Leadership

Self-aware leaders are better equipped to:
1. Recognize Biases: Understand and mitigate personal biases that may affect decision-making and interactions.
2. Manage Stress: Identify stress triggers and employ strategies to manage stress effectively.
3. Build Authentic Relationships: Engage with team members in a genuine and transparent manner.

Chapter 5: Active Listening and Communication

The Importance of Active Listening

Active listening is a critical skill for empathetic leaders. It involves fully concentrating on the speaker, understanding their message, and responding thoughtfully. Active listening helps leaders understand their team members' needs, concerns, and ideas.

Techniques for Active Listening

1. Give Full Attention: Eliminate distractions and focus entirely on the speaker.
2. Show Interest: Use verbal and non-verbal cues to show that you are engaged, such as nodding and maintaining eye contact.
3. Reflect and Clarify: Paraphrase what the speaker has said to ensure understanding and ask clarifying questions.
4. Avoid Interrupting: Let the speaker finish their thoughts before responding.

Effective Communication Strategies

Empathetic leaders communicate clearly, respectfully, and with consideration for their audience's emotions and perspectives. Strategies include:

1. Being Transparent: Share information openly and honestly to build trust.
2. Using Positive Language: Frame messages in a positive and encouraging manner.
3. Encouraging Feedback: Create an environment where team members feel comfortable providing input and expressing concerns.

Chapter 6: Building Trust and Authentic Relationships

The Foundation of Trust

Trust is essential for effective leadership. Empathetic leaders build trust by being consistent, reliable, and showing genuine care for their team members.

Building Authentic Relationships

Authentic relationships are built on mutual respect, honesty, and understanding. Empathetic leaders:

1. Show Genuine Interest: Take the time to learn about team members' interests, goals, and challenges.
2. Be Vulnerable: Share your own experiences and challenges to create a sense of shared humanity.
3. Provide Support: Offer assistance and resources to help team members achieve their goals.

Maintaining Trust and Authenticity

Maintaining trust requires ongoing effort and integrity. Empathetic leaders:

1. Follow Through: Keep promises and commitments to demonstrate reliability.
2. Admit Mistakes: Acknowledge and learn from mistakes to show humility and accountability.
3. Respect Privacy: Handle sensitive information with discretion and respect.

Chapter 7: Emotional Intelligence in Leadership

Understanding Emotional Intelligence

Emotional intelligence (EI) is the ability to recognize, understand, and manage your own emotions, as well as the emotions of others. It comprises four key components:

1. Self-Awareness: Recognizing and understanding your own emotions.
2. Self-Management: Regulating your emotions and behaviors.
3. Social Awareness: Understanding others' emotions and perspectives.
4. Relationship Management: Building and maintaining healthy relationships.

Enhancing Emotional Intelligence

Leaders can develop their EI through:

1. Self-Reflection: Regularly assess your emotional responses and behaviors.

2. Empathy Practices: Engage in activities that enhance your ability to understand and share others' feelings.
3. Stress Management: Develop strategies to manage stress effectively.
4. Interpersonal Skills: Improve your communication, conflict resolution, and teamwork skills.

The Impact of EI on Leadership

Leaders with high EI are better equipped to:

1. Navigate Complex Situations: Handle challenging situations with composure and insight.
2. Inspire and Motivate: Connect with team members on an emotional level to inspire and motivate them.
3. Resolve Conflicts: Address conflicts with empathy and understanding, leading to more effective resolutions.

Chapter 8: Fostering a Positive Work Environment

Creating a Culture of Respect and Inclusion

Empathetic leaders cultivate a work environment where respect and inclusion are paramount. This involves:

1. Promoting Diversity: Encourage diverse perspectives and backgrounds within the team.
2. Inclusive Practices: Implement policies and practices that ensure all team members feel valued and included.
3. Open Communication: Foster a culture where open and honest communication is encouraged.

Recognizing and Rewarding Effort

Acknowledging and rewarding team members' efforts and achievements fosters a positive and motivating work environment. Empathetic leaders:

1. Give Praise: Regularly recognize and praise team members for their contributions.
2. Provide Opportunities: Offer opportunities for growth and development.
3. Celebrate Successes: Celebrate both individual and team successes to build a sense of camaraderie and achievement.

Supporting Work-Life Balance

Empathetic leaders understand the importance of work-life balance and strive to support their team members in achieving it. Strategies include:

1. Flexible Work Arrangements: Offer flexible work hours and remote work options.
2. Encouraging Breaks: Promote regular breaks and time off to prevent burnout.
3. Providing Resources: Offer resources and support for mental and physical well-being.

Chapter 9: Empathy in Decision Making

The Role of Empathy in Decision Making

Empathetic leaders incorporate empathy into their decision-making processes to ensure that their choices consider the well-being and perspectives of their team members.

Strategies for Empathetic Decision Making

1. Gather Input: Seek input from team members to understand their views and concerns.
2. Consider Impact: Evaluate the potential impact of decisions on team members and stakeholders.
3. Communicate Transparently: Clearly communicate the rationale behind decisions and how they align with the team's values and goals.

Balancing Empathy with Accountability

While empathy is crucial, leaders must also balance it with accountability and performance. This involves:

1. Setting Clear Expectations: Define clear expectations and goals for the team.
2. Providing Constructive Feedback: Offer feedback that is both supportive and focused on improvement.
3. Holding Team Members Accountable: Ensure that team members are held accountable for their responsibilities and performance.

Chapter 10: Challenges and Pitfalls

Common Challenges in Empathetic Leadership

Empathetic leaders may face several challenges, including:

1. Balancing Empathy and Authority: Maintaining authority while being empathetic can be challenging.
2. Emotional Drain: Continuously empathizing with others can be emotionally draining.
3. Managing Diverse Needs: Addressing the diverse needs and concerns of team members can be complex.

Overcoming Challenges

Strategies to overcome these challenges include:

1. Setting Boundaries: Establish clear boundaries to manage your emotional energy and prevent burnout.

2. Delegating Responsibility: Delegate tasks and responsibilities to balance workload and maintain authority.
3. Continuous Learning: Engage in ongoing learning and development to enhance your empathetic leadership skills.

Avoiding Pitfalls

Common pitfalls to avoid include:

1. Over-Identification: Avoid becoming too emotionally involved in team members' issues, which can impair objectivity.
2. Neglecting Self-Care: Prioritize self-care to maintain your own well-being and effectiveness as a leader.
3. Inconsistent Application: Ensure that empathy is consistently applied in all interactions and decisions.

Chapter 11: Sustaining Empathetic Leadership

Continuous Improvement

Sustaining empathetic leadership requires a commitment to continuous improvement. This involves:

1. Seeking Feedback: Regularly seek feedback from team members and colleagues to identify areas for improvement.
2. Reflecting on Practices: Reflect on your leadership practices and make adjustments as needed.
3. Staying Informed: Stay informed about new research and best practices in empathetic leadership.

Building a Support Network

Empathetic leaders benefit from a strong support network that includes:

1. Mentors and Coaches: Seek guidance and support from mentors and leadership coaches.
2. Peer Support: Connect with other empathetic leaders to share experiences and insights.
3. Professional Development: Engage in professional development opportunities to enhance your skills and knowledge.

Leading by Example

Empathetic leaders set an example for their team by embodying the principles of empathy in their actions and decisions. This involves:

1. Demonstrating Empathy: Consistently demonstrate empathy in your interactions with team members.
2. Encouraging Empathy in Others: Encourage and support team members in developing and practicing empathy.
3. Creating a Legacy: Strive to create a lasting legacy of empathy and compassion within your organization.

Conclusion

Empathetic leadership is a transformative approach that fosters a positive, inclusive, and productive work environment. By understanding and practicing empathy, leaders can build stronger relationships, enhance team collaboration, and drive organizational success. This book has provided you with the tools and insights needed to become an empathetic leader and make a meaningful impact on your team and organization. As you continue on your leadership journey, remember that empathy is a powerful force for positive change.

www.ingramcontent.com/pod-product-compliance
Lightning Source LLC
Chambersburg PA
CBHW050255230526
45470CB00005B/2280